Commissioned by the Spokane Symphony Orchestra

Eckart Preu, Music Director

in consortium with the Elgin Symphony Orchestra

in celebration of the 200th anniversary of Abraham Lincoln's birth

World premiere by Spokane Symphony Orchestra

Thomas Hampson, baritone, Eckart Preu conducting

at the Martin Woldson Theater at The Fox

Spokane, Washington

February 28, 2009

First recorded by Spokane Symphony Orchestra

Thomas Hampson, baritone, Eckart Preu conducting

On E1 Music, EIE-CD-7725

Full score for sale through Hal Leonard

ISMN 979-0-051-09764-7

Performance materials are available from the

Boosey & Hawkes Rental Library

ABRAHAM LINCOLN BIOGRAPHY

Born in 1809 in a one-room log cabin in rural Kentucky to uneducated, poor farmers, Abraham Lincoln was able teach himself how to read, write, and do arithmetic by reading Shakespeare, poetry, newspapers, and books on philosophy and mathematics. He also taught himself how to play the violin and harmonica, became a champion wrestler, and was handy with an axe. That he eventually became President of the United States from such humble beginnings has baffled biographers ever since.

As a young man in Illinois, he practiced law by driving a horse and buggy across the Midwest prairie from town to town where he earned the nickname "Honest Abe." There he became a successful lawyer and politician who could dazzle a crowd with his witty comments, humorous stories, and theatrical way of delivering a speech. At the same time, Lincoln was a loner who could sit for hours at time in deep thought, "wrapped in abstraction and gloom." If he went to a concert, lecture or minstrel show, "he would just as soon go alone." Although Lincoln was a spiritual man who often quoted the Bible and frequently made use of biblical images in his writings, he never joined a church.

As a young man in New Salem, Illinois, he fell in love with Anne Rutledge and never recovered from her untimely death at the age of 22. In 1842, Lincoln reluctantly married the high-strung and temperamental Mary Todd (1818-1882), a decision which haunted him the rest of his life.

After only a two-year term as congressman from Illinois in the United States House of Representatives, the widely unknown and untested Lincoln was elected the 16th President of the United States at a time when the country was at the brink of Civil War (1860-1865). With little military experience, Lincoln became the Commander-in-Chief of the Union army in this "bloody war." He did not hesitate to use violent force when necessary, and micromanaged the battle strategies of his generals and their battles. Yet Lincoln was a peaceful man who believed in solving conflict with "peaceful ballots" and not "bloody bullets": he never fired a shot as a young man in the Blackhawk Indian War, and he was against the hunting of animals with firearms.

After being re-elected to a second term as President, only days after General Robert E. Lee surrendered his Confederate army to General Ulysses S. Grant, Lincoln, who was eager to begin the peaceful reunification of a war torn country, was assassinated on April 15, 1865.

MICHAEL DAUGHERTY

LETTERS FROM LINCOLN

FOR BARITONE AND ORCHESTRA
(2009)

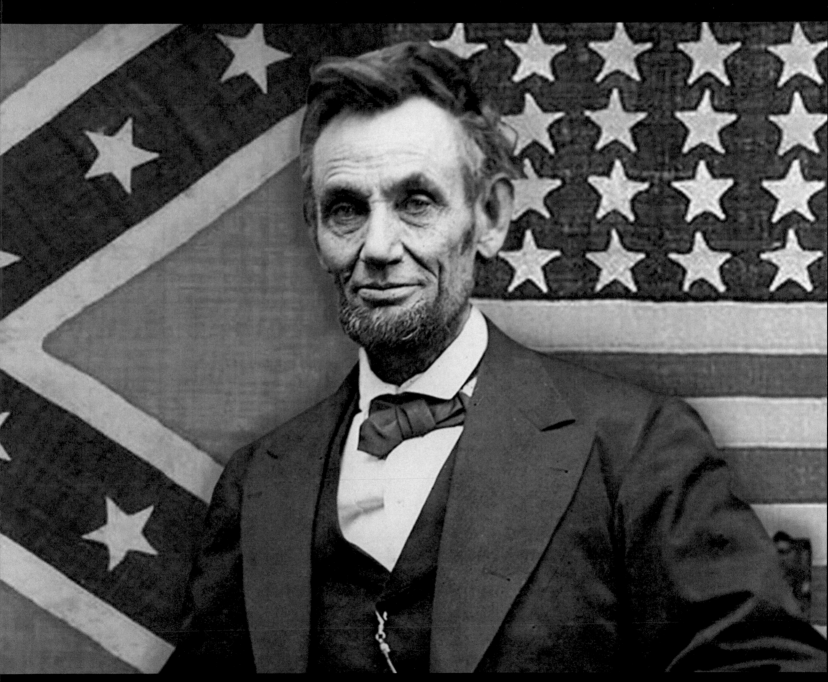

HENDON MUSIC

BOOSEY & HAWKES

AN IMAGEM COMPANY

DISTRIBUTED BY

HAL•LEONARD®
CORPORATION
7777 W. BLUEMOUND RD. P.O. BOX 13819 MILWAUKEE, WI 53213

www.boosey.com
www.halleonard.com

Published by Hendon Music, Inc.
a Boosey & Hawkes company
229 West 28th Street, 11th Floor
New York NY 10001

www.boosey.com

ISMN 979-0-051-09765-4

Cover Image: Abraham Lincoln (2014) Peter Shin. Used by permission.
Photography: Abraham Lincoln, National Archives, Public Domain.

First printed April 2014
Music copying by Ian Dicke and Paul Dooley

COMPOSER'S BIOGRAPHY

Grammy® Award winning composer Michael Daugherty is one of the most commissioned, performed, and recorded composers on the American concert music scene today. His music is rich with cultural allusions and bears the stamp of classic modernism, with colliding tonalities and blocks of sound; at the same time, his melodies can be eloquent and stirring. Daugherty has been hailed by *The Times* (London) as "a master icon maker" with a "maverick imagination, fearless structural sense and meticulous ear."

Daugherty first came to international attention when the Baltimore Symphony Orchestra, conducted by David Zinman, performed his *Metropolis Symphony* at Carnegie Hall in 1994. Since that time, Daugherty's music has entered the orchestral, band and chamber music repertory and made him, according to the League of American Orchestras, one of the ten most performed American composers. In 2011, the Nashville Symphony's Naxos recording of Daugherty's *Metropolis Symphony* and *Deus ex Machina* was honored with three Grammy® Awards, including Best Classical Contemporary Composition.

Born in 1954 in Cedar Rapids, Iowa, Daugherty is the son of a dance-band drummer and the oldest of five brothers, all professional musicians. He studied music composition at the University of North Texas (1972-76), the Manhattan School of Music (1976-78), and computer music at Pierre Boulez's IRCAM in Paris (1979-80). Daugherty received his doctorate from Yale University in 1986 where his teachers included Jacob Druckman, Earle Brown, Roger Reynolds, and Bernard Rands. During this time, he also collaborated with jazz arranger Gil Evans in New York, and pursued further studies with composer György Ligeti in Hamburg, Germany (1982-84). After teaching music composition from 1986-90 at the Oberlin Conservatory of Music, Daugherty joined the School of Music at the University of Michigan (Ann Arbor) in 1991, where he is Professor of Composition and a mentor to many of today's most talented young composers.

Daugherty has been Composer-in-Residence with the Louisville Symphony Orchestra (2000), Detroit Symphony Orchestra (1999-2003), Colorado Symphony Orchestra (2001-02), Cabrillo Festival of Contemporary Music (2001-04, 2006-08, 2011), Westshore Symphony Orchestra (2005-06), Eugene Symphony (2006), Henry Mancini Summer Institute (2006), Music from Angel Fire Chamber Music Festival (2006), Pacific Symphony (2010-11), Chattanooga Symphony (2012-13), New Century Chamber Orchestra (2013), and Albany Symphony (2015).

Daugherty has received numerous awards, distinctions, and fellowships for his music, including: a Fulbright Fellowship (1977), the Kennedy Center Friedheim Award (1989), the Goddard Lieberson Fellowship from the American Academy of Arts and Letters (1991), fellowships from the National Endowment for the Arts (1992) and the Guggenheim Foundation (1996), and the Stoeger Prize from the Chamber Music Society of Lincoln Center (2000). In 2005, Daugherty received the Lancaster Symphony Orchestra Composer's Award, and in 2007, the Delaware Symphony Orchestra selected Daugherty as the winner of the A.I. DuPont Award. Also in 2007, he received the American Bandmasters Association Ostwald Award for his composition *Raise the Roof* for Timpani and Symphonic Band. Daugherty has been named "Outstanding Classical Composer" at the Detroit Music Awards in 2007, 2009 and 2010. His GRAMMY® award winning recordings can be heard on Albany, Argo, Delos, Equilibrium, Klavier, Naxos and Nonesuch labels.

Abraham Lincoln (February 12, 1809 – April 15, 1865)

16th President of the United States

COMPOSER'S NOTE

Letters from Lincoln (2009) for baritone and orchestra was commissioned by the Spokane Symphony, Eckart Preu, Music Director, in consortium with the Elgin Symphony Orchestra, in celebration of the 200th anniversary of Abraham Lincoln's birth (February 12, 1809). The world premiere was given by the Spokane Symphony under the direction of Eckart Preu, with Thomas Hampson, baritone, at the Martin Woldson Theatre at the Fox, Spokane, Washington on February 28, 2009. The work is 25 minutes in length and scored for baritone solo, piccolo, flute, oboe, English horn, clarinet, bass clarinet, bassoon, contrabassoon, 2 horns, 2 trumpets, 2 trombones, timpani, two percussion, harp and strings.

Historians and the public generally regard Lincoln as America's greatest president, who successfully led the United States through the Civil War and initiated the end of slavery. His life, which was full of spectacular opposites, ironies, contradictions and pathos, provided me with abundance of musical dramatic possibilities.

While composing this musical work inspired by Lincoln, I discovered ways to bring his historic greatness into the present. I read Lincoln's speeches, poems and letters, and studied his life; I visited the Lincoln Memorial in Washington D.C., and I traveled to the battlefields of Gettysburg.

Lincoln's impassioned writings, from his youth as poor boy in the backwoods of Kentucky to his tragic death as President of the United States, have moved me to take his own words, both public and private, and set them to song. In *Letters from Lincoln*, I create a musical portrait of a man who expressed his vision with eloquence, and with hope that the human spirit could overcome prejudice and differences of opinion in order to create a better world.

—Michael Daugherty

TEXT by ABRAHAM LINCOLN

II. Autobiography (December 20, 1859, Illinois)

I was born February 12, 1809, in Kentucky.
I am, in height, six feet, four inches; weighing on an average one hundred and eighty pounds;
dark complexion, with coarse black hair, and grey eyes.

III. Abraham Lincoln is My Name (1824-26, Indiana)

Abraham Lincoln is my name
And with my pen I wrote the same

I wrote in both haste and speed
And left it here for fools to read

Abraham Lincoln his hand and pen
He will be good but God knows when

Swift as an Indian arrow
Fly like a shooting star

If I were two-faced, would I be wearing this one?

IV. The Mystic Chords of Memory (March 4, 1861, Washington D.C.)

Bloody conflict
Bloody fields
Bloody code
Bloody war

A house divided against itself cannot stand

Bloody bullets
Bloody bones
Bloody hand
Bloody war

Not bloody bullets, but peaceful ballots
We are not enemies, but friends

The mystic chords of memory, stretching from every battlefield and patriot grave to every living
heart and hearthstone all over this broad land, will yet swell the chorus of the Union, when again
touched, as surely they will be, by the better angels of our nature.

V. Letter to Mrs. Bixby (November 21, 1864, Washington D.C.)

I have been shown in the files of the War Department that you are the mother of five sons who have died in the field of battle.

I feel how weak must be any word of mine which should attempt to beguile you from the grief of a loss so overwhelming.

I pray that our Heavenly Father may assuage the anguish of your bereavement, and leave you only the cherished memory of the loved and lost, and the solemn pride that must be yours to have laid so costly a sacrifice upon the altar of freedom.

Yours, very sincerely and respectfully,
A. Lincoln

VI. Mrs. Lincoln's Music Box (June 9, 1863, Washington, D.C)

Telegram to Mrs. Lincoln:
I think you better put "Tad's" pistol away. I had an ugly dream about him.

VII. Gettysburg Address (November 19, 1863, Pennsylvania)

Four score and seven years ago our fathers brought forth on this continent, a new nation, conceived in Liberty, and dedicated to the proposition that all men are created equal.

Now we are engaged in a great civil war, testing whether that nation, or any nation so conceived and so dedicated, can long endure. We are met on a great battle-field of that war. We have come to dedicate a portion of that field, as a final resting place for those who here gave their lives that that nation might live. It is altogether fitting and proper that we should do this.

But, in a larger sense, we cannot dedicate – we cannot consecrate – we cannot hallow – this ground. The brave men, living and dead, who struggled here, have consecrated it, far above our poor power to add or detract. The world will little note, nor long remember what we say here, but it can never forget what they did here. It is for us the living, rather, to be dedicated here to the unfinished work which they who fought here have thus far so nobly advanced. It is rather for us to be here dedicated to the great task remaining before us – that from these honored dead we take increased devotion to that cause for which they gave the last full measure of devotion – that we here highly resolve that these dead shall not have died in vain – that this nation, under God, shall have a new birth of freedom – and that government of the people, by the people, for the people, shall not perish from the earth.

STAGE ARRANGEMENT

I. Lincoln's Funeral Train
VI. Mrs. Lincoln's Music Box
VII. Gettysburg Address

Trumpet 1   Percussion   Trumpet 2
Stage right   Stage left
Stand to play   Stand to play

                              Orchestra

                              Conductor

            Baritone

CONTENTS

INSTRUMENTATION

Flute
Piccolo (doubling Flute)
Oboe
English horn
B♭ Clarinet
Bass Clarinet
Bassoon
Contrabassoon

2 Horns in F
2 Trumpets in C
2 Trombones (2. Bass Trombone)

Timpani (five drums)

Percussion (two players; instruments are not shared unless indicated otherwise)

1. Triangle, Chimes, Glockenspiel, Xylophone, Medium Suspended Cymbal (cello bow),
Bass Drum (shared with Perc. 2), Large Whip (shared with Perc. 2),
2 Flexatones (one for each hand)

2. Triangle, Washboard (scrape with metal thimble), Piccolo Snare Drum,
Large Suspended Cymbal (cello bow), Large Mark Tree,
Bass Drum (shared with Perc. 1), Large Whip (shared with Perc. 1),

Harp

Baritone (range: B - g')

Strings

Duration: *ca.* 25 minutes

Score in C

Commissioned by the Spokane Symphony, Eckart Preu, Music Director,
in consortium with the Elgin Symphony Orchestra,
in celebration of the 200th anniversary of Abraham Lincoln's birth

LETTERS FROM LINCOLN

ABRAHAM LINCOLN
(1809–1865)

Vocal part edited by
THOMAS HAMPSON

MICHAEL DAUGHERTY
(2009)

Piano Reduction
by the Composer

I. Lincoln's Funeral Train

(April 15 – May 4, 1865, Washington, D.C. – Springfield, Illinois)

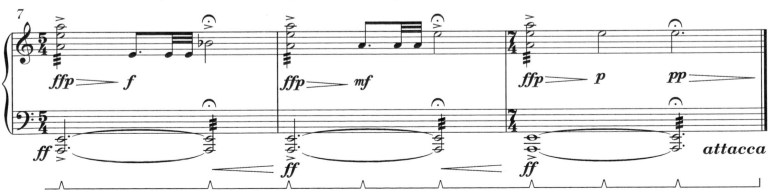

979-0-051-09765-4

II. Autobiography

(December 20, 1859, Springfield, Illinois)

attacca

III. Abraham Lincoln is My Name

(1824 – 26, Indiana)

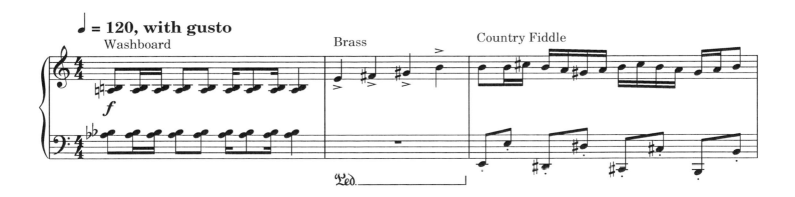

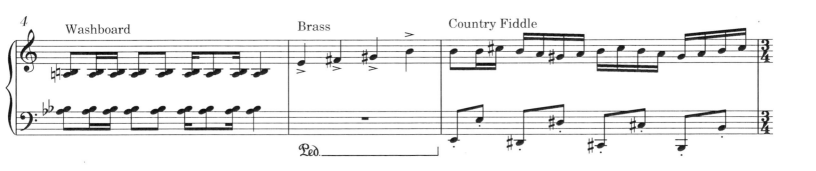

IV. Mystic Chords of Memory

(March 4, 1861, Washington, D.C.)

bones   Blood-y   hand   Blood-y   war

F ♩ = 52, quasi recitativo

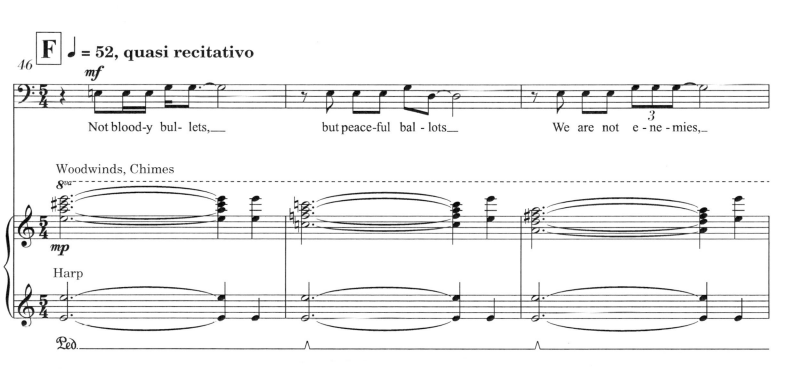

Not blood-y bul- lets,___   but peace-ful bal - lots___   We are not e - ne - mies,___

Woodwinds, Chimes

Harp

rit.   *mp*   a tempo

but_____ friends

L.H.

Strings

p legato

con Ped.

Bells, Clarinet,
Cello, Double Bass

The my-stic chords of mem-o-ry,___ stretch-ing from eve-ry bat-tle-field

to eve-ry liv-ing heart all o-ver this broad___ land,

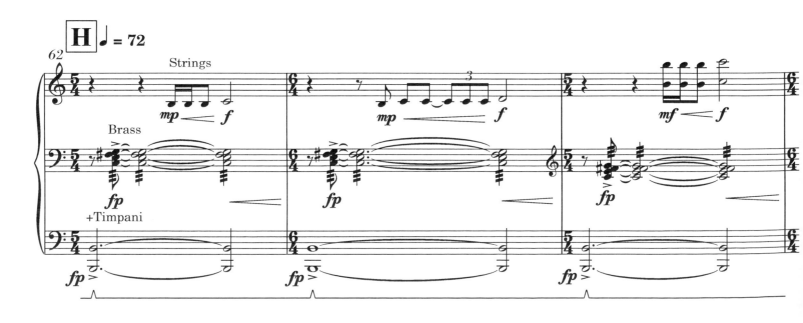

V. Letter to Mrs. Bixby

(November 21, 1864, Washington, D.C.)

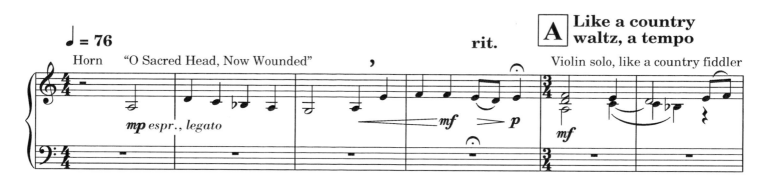

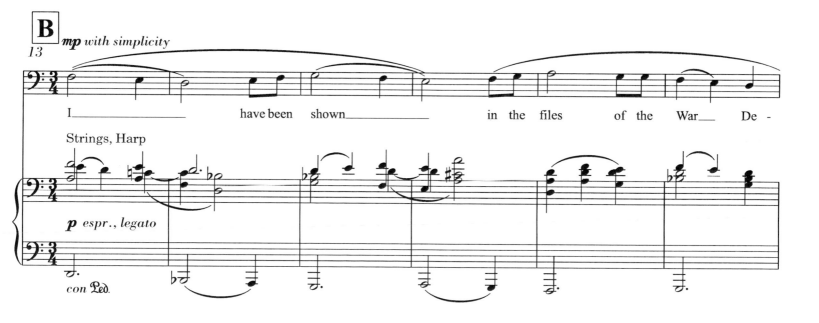

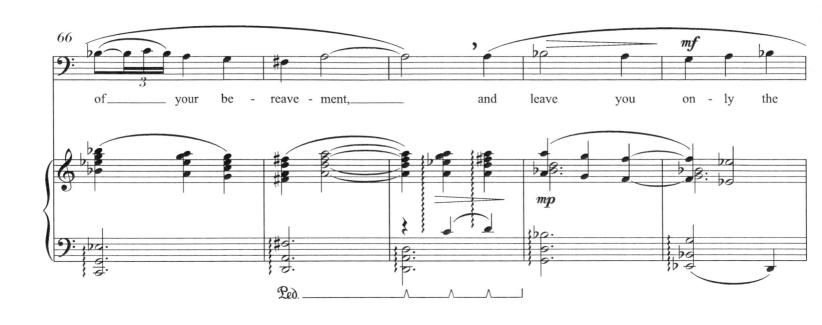

of ___ your be - reave - ment, ___ and leave you on - ly the

cher - ished mem - o - ry of the loved ___ and lost, ___

and the sol - - -

Woodwinds
"O Sacred Head, Now Wounded"

Horn

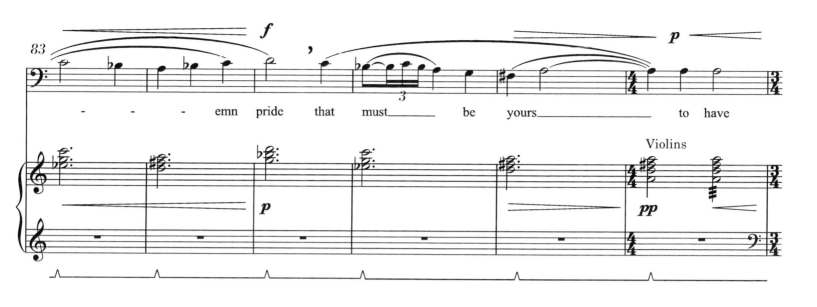

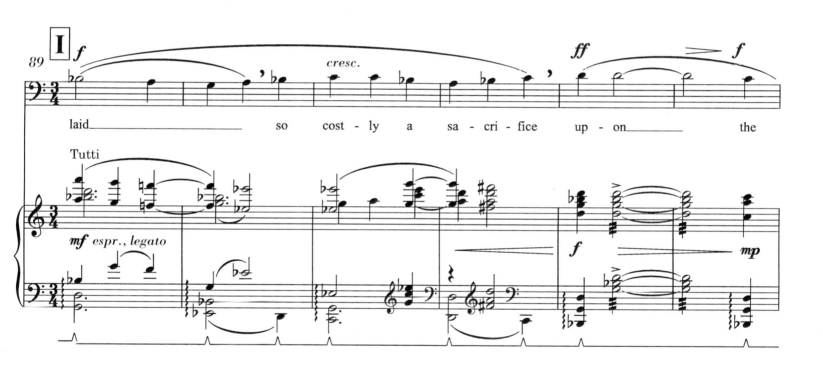

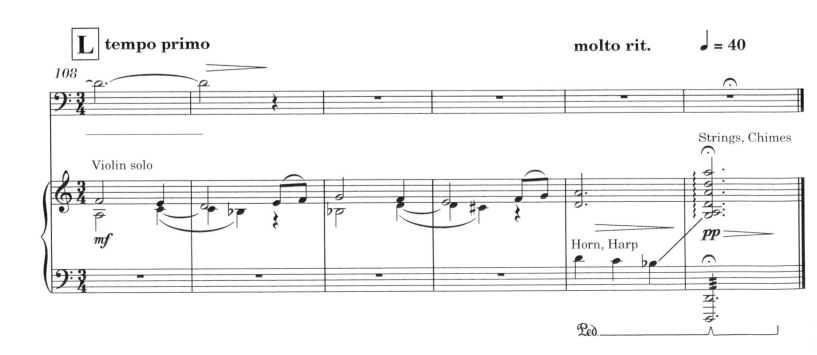

VI. Mrs. Lincoln's Music Box

(June 9, 1863, Washington, D.C.)

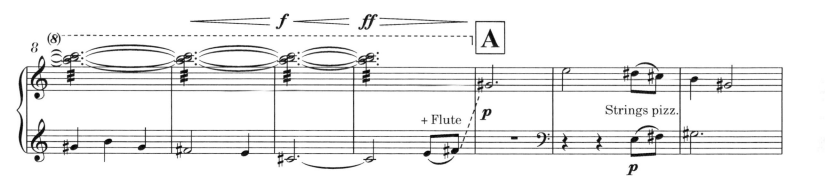

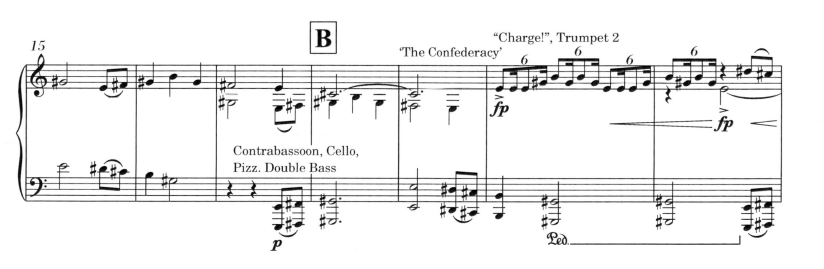

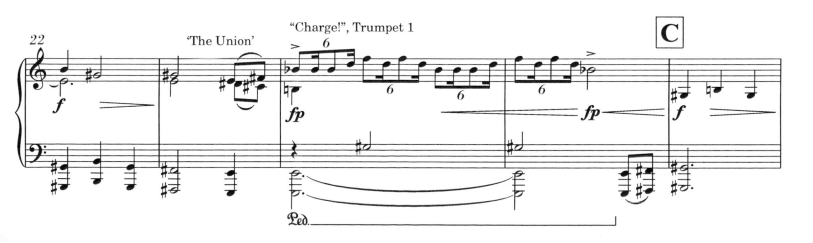

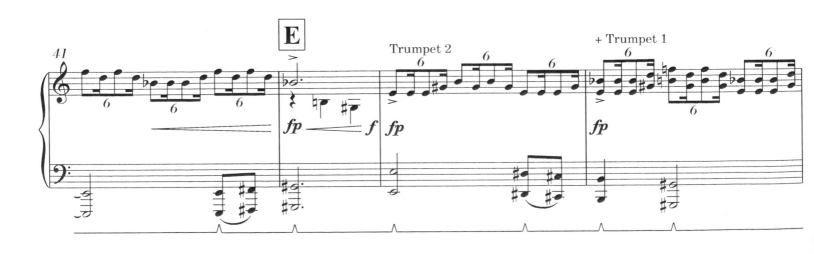

Telegram to Mrs. Lincoln:

I think you bet - ter put "Tad's" pis - tol a - way.__ I__

Flexatone, Strings (as high as possible)
(a♮, b♭, b♮, c♮)

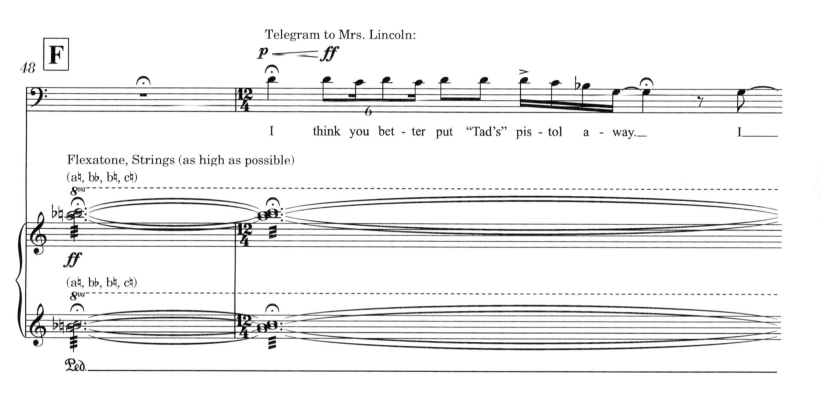

col canto _____ as high as possible

gliss.   gliss.   gliss.

__ had an ug - ly dream a - bout him.__

(a♮, b♭, b♮, c♮)

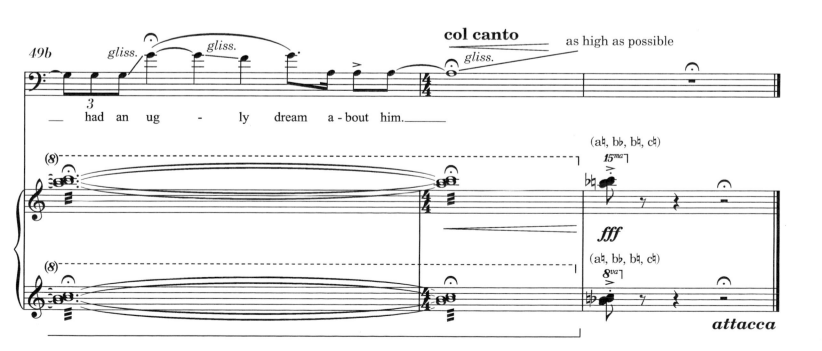

attacca

VII. Gettysburg Address

(November 19, 1863, Pennsylvania)

that we here high - ly re - solve   that these dead   shall not have

died in vain– that this na - tion, un - der God,

shall have a new birth of free - dom   and that gov - ern - ment

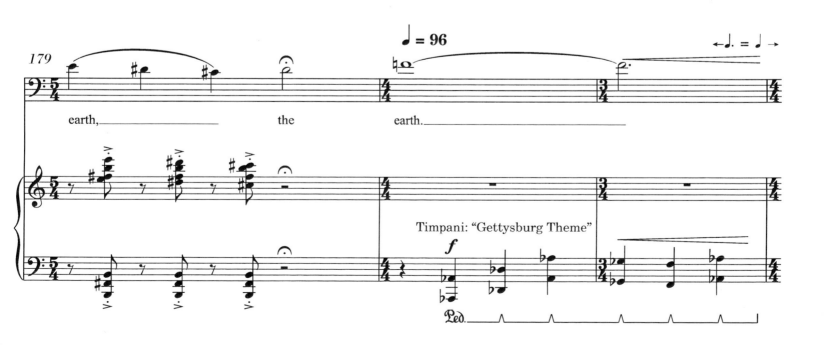

Con 🎵 Ped.

*In performance, the pianist should play the lower two staves at ⑤.

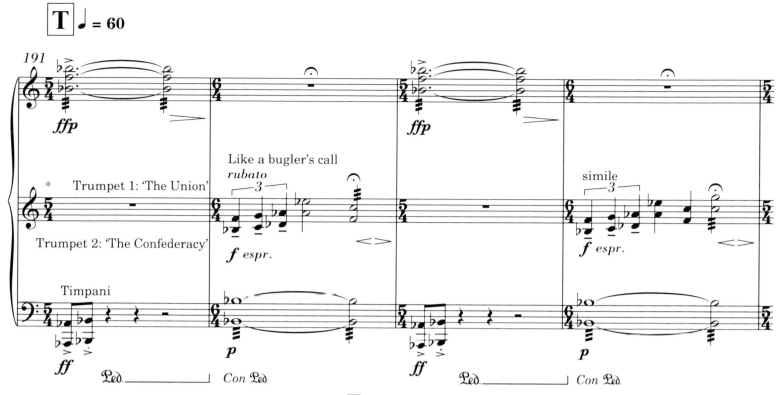

*In performance, the pianist should play all three staves at $\boxed{\text{T}}$.

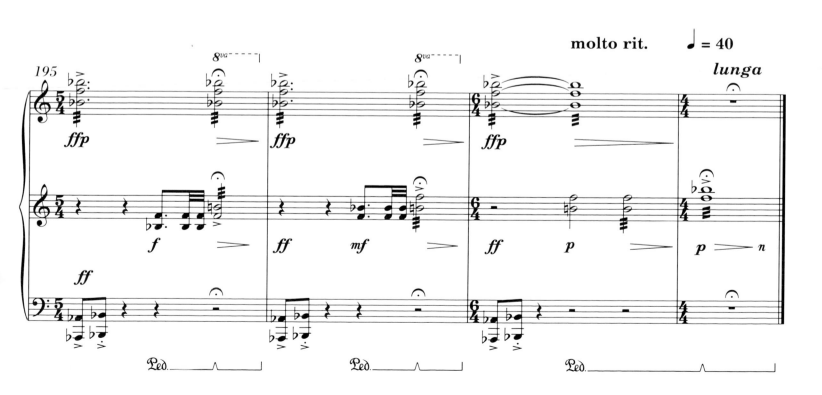

Fine